PUBLISHED BY

Kirkbymoorside History Group 2014

COPYRIGHT © KIRKBYMOORSIDE HISTORY GROUP 2014

ISBN 978-0-9564745-8-2

PRINTED BY

HPE PRINT
THORNTON ROAD
INDUSTRIAL ESTATE
PICKERING
NORTH YORKSHIRE
YO18 7JB
TEL: 01751 473578

Kathleen Emily Dowson

Kathleen Dowson's Family Tree

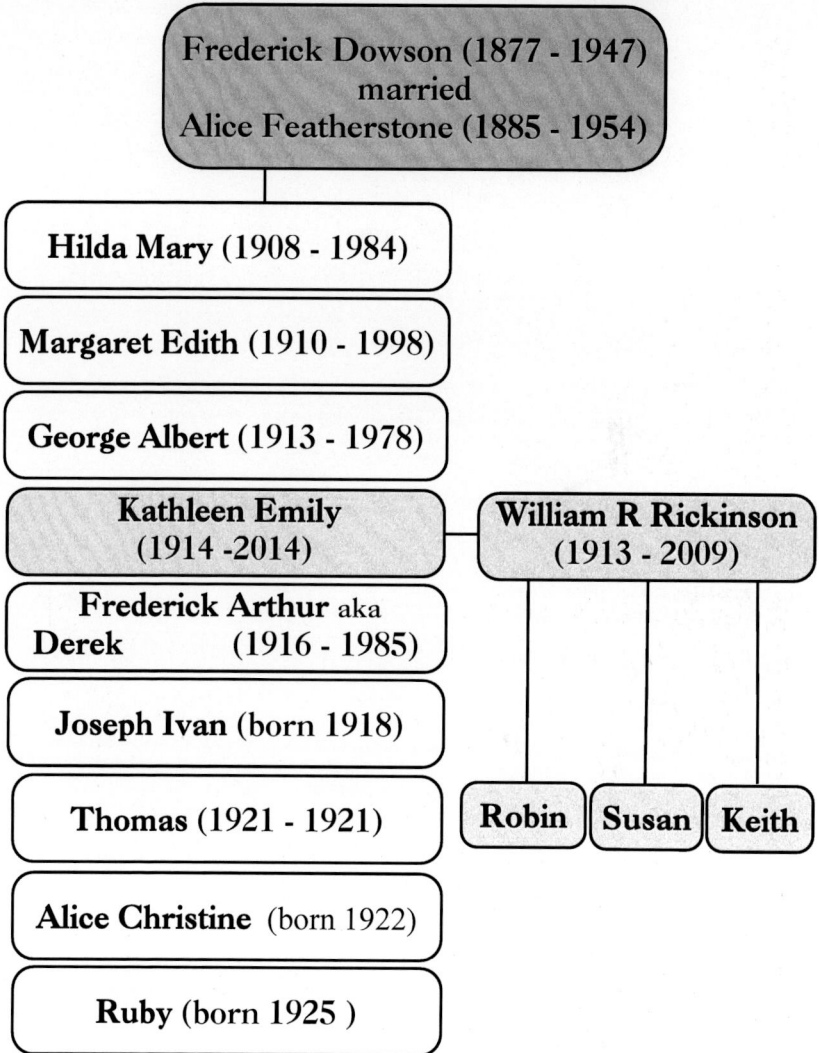

Frederick Dowson (1877 - 1947)
married
Alice Featherstone (1885 - 1954)

Hilda Mary (1908 - 1984)

Margaret Edith (1910 - 1998)

George Albert (1913 - 1978)

Kathleen Emily (1914 -2014) — William R Rickinson (1913 - 2009)

Frederick Arthur aka Derek (1916 - 1985)

Joseph Ivan (born 1918)

Thomas (1921 - 1921)

Robin | Susan | Keith

Alice Christine (born 1922)

Ruby (born 1925)

Two Dowson children in Gillamoor in the 1900s

Auntie Kath Recalls A Kirkby Childhood

Kathleen Dowson was born in Gillamoor in 1914 and moved to Kirkbymoorside around the age of three. Her father was Frederick Dowson, who came from a family of blacksmiths whilst her grandfather, Joseph, had a forge in Piercy End.

Fred moved up to Gillamoor and ran a blacksmith's and shoeing shop. Kath's mother was Alice Featherstone, whose family came from Fadmoor. They initially lived in Gillamoor, with the Simpson family as neighbours at one side and the Ainsley family on the other; Margaret Ainsley was the schoolmistress in Gillamoor. However, the family moved into Kirkbymoorside around 1917 with Fred continuing to work in Gillamoor.

The Featherstones were a farming family, and a complicated one at that. Kath's grandfather, Thomas Potter Featherstone, had two families. His first wife - Margaret (neé Petch) - who was Alice's mother, died in 1894 leaving behind five children. Thomas married again, to Louisa Walker in 1897, and went on to have another eight children with her.

Alice and Fred had nine children, losing a son, Thomas, in infancy in 1921. Kathleen was the fourth child, born between two brothers - Derek and Albert - to whom she was close. Despite the challenges of a large family, they were all brought up in a two storey terraced house in Dale End.

On leaving school Kath moved onto Scarborough to work for the Pickup and Hesleton families as a mother's help and nanny, where she met her future husband William (Bill).

Kath married William Rickinson in 1938 and with the start of the Second World War, the couple moved to the Bradford area.

Bill joined up at the start of WWII with the Royal Corps Signals as a despatch rider based in Chester. He was discharged soon after due to hearing problems. Both Bill and Kath worked with the Forestry in the Ripon area, loading pit props into lorries by hand. However the physical work took its toll and she developed a hernia meaning she could no longer work there. So they moved to Bradford where both Bill and Kath worked 12 hour shifts, seven days a week in a munitions factory. When the sirens went off, neither of them had the energy to go down to the shelter and would rather die in their beds.

Their house at the time was about two miles out of the town centre, near the reservoir, which the German planes used as a marker to locate the town and drop incendiary bombs. One dropped on the Odeon cinema, shortly after the couple had left, destroying the interior completely but leaving the walls intact.

One weekend they decided to go visit friends in Clapham and went down on the train. During their first night there, bombs fell at the end of the street. There was no shelter so they ended up hiding under the bed all night. Their friend, Bert, who was an ARP Warden, came home that morning with the smell of death about him. He had spent all night removing dead bodies from the bomb craters and so they decided to return home straight away. Although Bradford was targeted, it was nothing compared to London's suffering.

Back in Bradford, Bill went to Bradford Infirmary for an operation to try and improve his hearing. Kath remembered how Bill complained how loud the Tetley's dray horse sounded, with it's iron shoes on the cobbled streets - it was deafening!

Bill and Kathleen's Wedding Day, 1938

However the hearing didn't last and he refused to go back to try again. This was partly because of one experience there. Whilst he was in, he saw a row of children all wrapped up in green plastic, waiting to have their tonsils out. It reminded him of a slaughterhouse and he was so horrified, he would never return.

In 1943 Kath moved back to Scarborough where their first son Robin was born. In 1945 Kath's daughter Susan was born followed by a son Keith in 1946. After the war ,the couple moved to Leeds and then back to Scarborough; Bill worked as a cabinetmaker and joiner, before joining Plaxton's coach builders, whilst Kath brought up their three children. Their children went onto marry and gave them eight grandchildren and 15 great grandchildren, to whom Kath and Bill were a source of fondness and inspiration.

Married for over 70 years, Bill died in 2009 on his 96th birthday; Kath died in 2014 just six months short of being 100 years old.

The following recollections are taken from two interviews completed back in 2010, when Kath was 96 years old, affectionately known to all as 'Auntie Kath'. They give an impressive account of a childhood and townsfolk now long gone. All the detail came from memory which is remarkable, but are personal to her and subject to interpretation.

This is her account of her childhood experiences; we hope it does Kathleen justice.

Bill and Kathleen

Home Life

"My first memory of Dale End was going out into the back yard and looking for the dairy – back in Gillamoor we lived on a farm and so had cows, and pigs, as well as a pony and trap. As a child I couldn't understand that Dale End was a small terraced house with a narrow yard and only a wash-house across the way. Our house was one of four in a row, all of which shared an outside tap. The back yard was lovely white concrete and at the far end were the coal house and earth closets. Beyond that Cooks had an area where they kept pigs.

When Dad got up on a morning the first thing he had to do was to light the fire and put the kettle on before he could have a cup of tea. There were nine of us in the family, but not all of us lived in the house at the same time. I've no idea how Mum managed with such a small house and such a large family to feed. She had a large double enamel pan to make porridge in for breakfast during the winter. It had water in the bottom to heat the porridge in the top. She had to make it the night before; there was no time on a morning! Despite the struggle Mum had making ends meet, I was always healthy. From the age of five up to when I left school at 14 years old, I never missed a day through illness.

Dad had an allotment, where he could grow vegetables, and a farmer up in Gillamoor let him have two furrows in one of the fields. The farmer would plough it for him and Dad would grow potatoes; although it was always Derek and me who had to plant them. We had to put a potato in the row, stand on it, take a stride, then put in another and so on up and down the furrows.

Grand-dad Featherstone used to lend Dad a horse and cart so we could gather tree branches or go up onto the moors to dig peat from the beds to keep the fire in. The peat was stacked to let it dry a bit and then we brought it home in the cart. It made a lovely fire which lasted. Derek and I would 'go stickin'. We took a hessian bag and collected sticks, small branches; anything that would go on the fire.

Grannie Featherstone used to make us big jam pies and she always made her pastry with beef dripping.

It was so sweet and sickly I struggled to eat it. "Oo, thoo is't thin, honey!" was the greeting I got whenever I visited but we ate well. We never had sweets as such, but were very happy with the dinners Mum made.

For as long as I could remember there was always a pan of water on the fire, ready just in case. Of the six houses in our row, four were alike and none of them had a boiler; everything to be heated had to go on the fire. Such a waste of heat really. My sister Margaret, who lived at Nunnington, had a side boiler with her fire and it made such a difference to her.

Next door to us lived the Russells, who were very posh and had an inside sink and tap, which was fantastic in those days. I remember they used to have a Wesleyan Minister lodging with them – a Mr Britain – who struck me as a being a very handsome young man.

With the four houses sharing one tap, wash day, which was Monday, was always busy. In the row we had a spinster who lived alone, a mother and daughter, the third had a couple with just one child and then there were us - the Dowsons – nine children in all.

Because of the amount of washing and the constant supply of water needed, Mum always had to wash on a Tuesday. Every pot and bucket had to be filled with cold water ready to fill the copper, a task which fell to Derek and I every time. Of course it was boring waiting for all these things to fill up, so we would leave the tap running and go off and play. Every time Betsy Bowes, the old lady next door, would shout out "Look, they're wasting water again!" Mum had to light the fire under the copper first thing ready for the day

ahead. On Tuesday she would fill the peggy tubs and wash the clothing for the week using a wooden dolly. She always managed to hang everything out the back, as everyone else had done theirs the day before.

One time I came home from school and there were all the boys' and Dad's socks waiting to be washed. I was with a friend who was an only child and her parents' lived opposite us on Gillamoor Road. When she heard about all these socks she said "We have some lovely hot water left, would you like it?" It had been used, but only once, so we took it home in a bucket for Mum to use for the socks.

In the wash-house we had an old wooden bath and it would dry out and leak; so we had to leave it full of water the night before so it would swell up and seal itself up for wash day. As the houses were built together, Mum could air the sheets by hanging them against the parlour wall, because next door's fireplace was behind it and so was always lovely and warm to touch. We had a large press against it and Mum used to air

nappies and sheets easily in it after they had been hung outside to dry.

She never ironed the sheets; but I remember she had a charcoal iron which she would fill with hot embers to heat up. It was very heavy and clumsy to use. She had the flat irons, which were great if you had a good fire going. But if the fire was smoky, the iron would leave smudges on the clean washing. There used to be a guard to put over the flat iron which took some of the heat away, if Mum was doing something delicate. She used to rub the irons with Bath Brick, which cleaned them and make them smooth. We used it to clean up the steel knives as well.

But of course we didn't change our clothes as often as you do today. I mean there were five girls in the family. Can you image if we changed every day? That would be 35 pairs of knickers! A copper full of them! Anyway, we always wore dark green and navy blue knickers, none of these white frilly things. And our winter clothes could be worn all winter; our gym slip could last for weeks, especially if you wore an apron over it. Everything was cotton or wool; we didn't have all these man-made fibres which seem to attract and hold onto the dirt.

Sisters: Kath (left) age six, with Hilda (back) and Margaret, KMS School 1920

Our house had two bedrooms and an attic, which went the length of the house with another three beds in it. Derek Margaret and I slept up there, the two boys in the back room and Mum and Dad in the other with Ruby.

In the attic there was a big cot, which I slept in until I was about three or four; one of the beds had a beautifully carved wooden headboard, which curved up in the centre to a knob. We used to put a pillow on the curve and pretend we were riding a horse.

On a Sunday morning Mum and Dad used to shout and say "Come and look after Ruby" so I would go down and get into bed with them to look after Ruby, all four of us in together. Mum and Dad would have a lie in and I would be fascinated with the bedstead.

At the bottom it was made up of long rails and in between there were sections of mother of pearl with brass knobs on the top. The pieces of mother of pearl were beautiful and shone like jewels; reds, greens, blues – I would just lay there watching them sparkle in the sunlight.

We had no gas or electric in the streets when we first moved to Dale End. I seem to think I had just left school when they came. Instead there was a man who had to come round and light street lamps on a night and turn them off during the day. Our house was lit with oil lamps so there was always a dark circle on the ceiling above the lamp which hung in the room. It was a half day job for Mum to take down the lamps, clean the glass and trim the wick. They all had to re-filled and during winter they would be on for hours.

At bed-time I was never allowed a candle; Mum was always worried about fires. Instead I had a Kelly lamp, which was round on the bottom so if it was knocked over it righted itself. I had a tin painted red to set it in next to my bed.

Of course if I needed to go to the toilet in the night I had to take a candle outside. I hated it. On a night-time all along the path, these great big worms came up between the stones and I used to shine the candlelight at them to frighten them away. It was scary going down to the closet in the dark on your own.

When the Aladdin lamps came out, they were better and gave out a wonderful light, but you had to be careful because they had a mantle in them, which was ever so brittle and they had to be primed. We would go and get our paraffin from Auntie Jinnie's shop or we would take a can down to Dowson's to be filled.

How Mum managed with all of us in such a small house I really don't know. She was always cheerful and we were kept well-dressed. If ever someone came to school with a safety pin holding their coat together she would say, "Well perhaps his mum hasn't been shown how to fix it." She always thought the best of folk. We were taught how to knit and sew from being young. I would knit pink woollen vests for Ruby and Mum would take them and crochet beautiful edging lace onto them.

Mum had a brother called Albert. He went with a friend from Fadmoor to New South Wales in Australia in 1912. They kept in touch and because the businesses in Kirby were all family owned, the only option was farming or domestic work. My brother Albert hated the cold and the slump had begun for everyone. Prices were going up and life was going down for everyone. Dad found it hard to make a living. So Mum wrote to her brother and arranged for all of us to go over and join him in a family farming venture. She saved up £5 for Albert to go join his uncle and we were to follow.

I told all my friends we were going to live in Australia. However the farm Uncle Albert had planned to buy was too costly and so we never went. All my friends called me a liar, which upset me, but not as much as Albert being out there on his own. It was like he had died. He kept in touch with Mum, but when she died, we lost contact.

Kath and her sisters, Ruby and Christine

It wasn't until my daughter Susan wrote again to his last known address that we discovered he was in the same place, even after all those years.

I managed to go over to spend some time with him and it was wonderful. Sadly he died suddenly a couple of months before he could make the trip back to see us all in England.

Another thing I can clearly remember is Dad trying to light the acetylene lamp which hung from his bicycle. You had to unscrew the lamp, find the small bits of rock in the bottom, add water and screw it back together. The burner had two holes and you had to light it through these holes. They were very difficult to light and would often go out. I remember Mum shouting to put some more water in as Dad got increasingly cross when his lamp wouldn't work.

Fun And Games

As a girl I always loved being outside. I would pack up my sisters, Christine and Ruby, and take them up the Manor Vale for breakfast.

Manor Vale was a children's paradise in my day. The grass was short like a park, kept right by the sheep which grazed there. And it had beautiful hills to sledge down in winter or roll down in summer. I would go digging for yennits. They had a white flower and feathery leaves, a bit like a carrot. The nuts underneath were all brown and bumpy. We ate them with salt. There would be primroses to pick and wild violets, hazelnuts and up towards the golf course on the right was Smiddy Wood where we could find wild strawberries. If we wanted bilberries we had to leave Manor Vale and go along the 'stoth'. This was a track that went along the top of the bank from Surprise View, Gillamoor to Fadill Rigg. And whilst we were there, we would gather gale from the beds at Lowna.

And, back in Manor Vale of course, there was the Swinging Tree. Every child knew about the Swinging Tree. It was an old ash tree with branches touching the ground. If you ran up the hill and grabbed hold of a branch, you had to pull it right back and then jump – it would swing you right off the ground. And if you climbed up the trunk, it divided into two with one thinner branch. This one you could slide along and it bent down to touch the floor, so you could jump off and watch as it swung back up. It was fantastic.

In amongst the tree roots, which were covered with thick green moss, we would sit with our feet in the holes and play houses. We put a tray on our knees and, from the quarry nearby, we would gather up bits of old pot and glass. We made pies from soil, decorated with a daisy and had pretend tea-parties. We would eat the red stems of the newly growing hawthorn leaves, which we said was our 'bread and butter'.

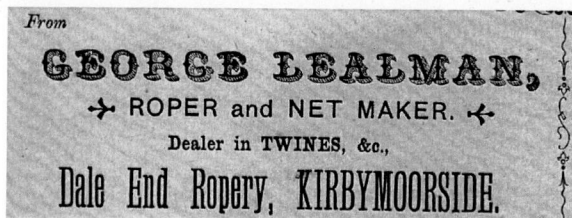

From

GEORGE LEALMAN,

✦ ROPER and NET MAKER. ✦

Dealer in **TWINES**, &c.,

Dale End Ropery, KIRBYMOORSIDE.

The rope walk was still there. We would watch Mr Lealman and his son making the ropes. I never really understood how they did it and as children we were not allowed to ask questions.

There was also the band hut, just before the gate. On a summer night when we had the bedroom windows open, we could hear the music as they practised on a Friday night; it was lovely.

My brothers and the other boys loved going into the caves in Manor Vale. You could get quite a way in, but I never dared. I always thought it had lions in there waiting for me. I suppose

I must have been told about the bones they found in the cave at Kirkdale and supposedly you could get all the way through at some time in the past.

On the other side of the rope walk the cave was better to get into and the lads would scramble in on their stomachs. That one led all the way up to a wooden door, that opened into the coal cellar in High Hall, in Castlegate. The Carters lived there when I was little. My friend Nora, her auntie, Gladys Hutchinson, worked there – all I remember about the house was that it was dingy inside. Low Hall was much nicer and statelier. Mrs Reveley and her daughter lived there; Miss Reveley was a piano teacher. Mum paid for my sister Margaret to have piano lessons, with the aim that she would teach me. But Margaret wasn't interested so I never got to learn.

I bet you've never heard a rhyme like this one; Mum taught it to us as little ones and I can still remember it:

> As I went over Umber Dumber, Umber
> Dumber Ony
> There I met Sir Rittamajig, taking away
> Compony

If I had my Itty Kitty, Itty Kitty Ony
I'd play up Sir Rittamajig for taking away
Compony!

It means - As I went over the hill (Umber Dumber) I met a
fox (Sir Rittamajig) who was stealing the goose (Compony)
and if I had had my gun (Itty Kitty) I would have shot him for
stealing the goose.

Mum had been taught it by her mother and grandmother,
but I don't know anyone else who's heard that rhyme
before.
When I went over to see my brother in Australia, he got me
to teach it to his grandchildren so it hasn't died out
completely.

We also had a strange clapping song we would sing, called
Santi Dor:

Santi Dor, Santi Dor, Santi Diddle-um a Diddle-um a Dor
There was a man who lived in Leeds,
He bought a garden full of seeds.
When the seeds began to grow, Like a garden full of snow.
When the snow began to melt, Like a ship without a belt.
When the ship began to sail, Like a bird without a tail.
When the bird began to fly, Like an eagle in the sky.
When the sky began to roar, Like a lion at my door.
When my door began to crack – All the ducks went quack,
quack, quack.

[Ed. This rhyme is almost identical to one listed in R Fairfax-
Blakeborough's book 'Yorkshire Wit, Character, Folklore &
Customs' 1898 (p.268-69). He traced it back into the 1700s but
that version has a more macabre ending:

And when my door began to crack
It was like a penknife at my back;
And when my back began to bleed,
I was dead, dead, dead indeed!

Kath knew nothing of this version and I only discovered it by chance after she had passed away.]

We had lots of other games to play like Beds – this was similar to Hop Scotch, but we drew eight squares on the pavement and you had to throw a ball into the first square (onesey) and bounce it once, then the second (which was twosey) and bounce it twice and so on until the eighth square. Each time you bounced the ball, you had to catch it before it hit the chalk line.

We used to play marbles or tors in the gutters – shuts and spans. The shut was when you sent the marble down and the span was how far it went. There is a saying 'like playing tors for nowt' which means a waste of time. And there were so many games you could play with a ball. Clapsey, where you had to bounce and clap before catching it; then you had to bounce the ball with one hand or on one leg so it got harder and harder.

We girls used to do a lot of skipping as well, with the two ropes. We would sing or chant things like 'What's the name of your young man?' and the person had to spell out the name whilst skipping. Another one was 'Where will you get married?' and we would say places like 'in a church, in a wheel barrow, in a muck cart'. There was always someone who tripped, as we got to muck cart and everyone would fall about laughing.

And I do remember the wood canters; big wagons pulled by horses, which carried trees and wood. They would be parked up opposite our house over the weekend. They had long poles at the back of the wagons and we would sit on them and bounce up and down.

B. & E. M. BLACKBURN
PROPRIETORS
ELECTRIC CINEMA
KIRBYMOORSIDE
Yorks.

There wasn't a cinema in my day, but there was a mobile one which set up in the Toll Booth on a Friday night. It would park round the back and they had an engine running to power the projector. Some people used to complain about the noise of this engine running all evening. It was all silent movies then; I remember they had a blind pianist who used to accompany the films. He lived in Kirby, but I can't remember his name. Nora Sample used to play sometimes as well as Ivy Blackburn. Mr Blackburn did the gas lamps. We all used to have to sit on wooden benches and if the film was a popular one, everyone ended up squashed together.

There were plenty of dances held in the Toll Booth as well as the cinema. I was a bit out of it really being one of the younger ones in the family; Hilda and Margaret were friends and had fellas; I was close to my brother Derek. We did everything together, so I really didn't go very often. Mum felt a bit sorry for me and got Margaret and her young man to take me to one dance.

I remember not knowing anyone and didn't know how to dance, but at the interval we went downstairs for refreshments and I saw all these dishes of jelly. They looked wonderful – red, green, orange – I couldn't believe my eyes! Margaret's boyfriend bought me one for 2d and it was fantastic – best bit of the evening. I didn't go to any more dances.

Of course, Margaret worked at the Pensioners Hospital on West Fields, when it had soldiers there. I remember seeing them outside on the beds, wearing their blue shirts. But I was only four when the WWI finished so don't remember much else.

Going into Town

I remember Mum never had time to go shopping so we always had to go off with the basket. One time, my sister Christine was going to recite her piece for the Chapel Anniversary and I desperately wanted a new hat. Well Mum couldn't go so I was sent to see the Miss Woods who had a haberdashery shop in the Market Place. They kindly put a selection of hats with the prices attached and let me bring them home so Mum could choose one and send the rest back. Everyone had to wear a hat for Chapel.

One incident I clearly remember was being sent by Mum to get some prunes from Gracie Jackson's shop, which was in Piercy End. Mum was always particular about our pronunciation – I was not allowed to speak in dialect. And so, as Kirby people used to say 'goin doon street' instead of 'going down street', I thought you had to say prowns instead of prunes. I was ever so embarrassed when Mrs Jackson said "Do you mean prunes, girl?"

Mrs Pot Isaacs had a shop opposite the blacksmiths in Piercy End, or as we knew it Railway Street. She was another strange lady and always put the letter 'h' on every word, even if it wasn't needed. And Thad Sleightholme sold tobacco nearby. Everyone except Mum and I smoked in our family. Dad and Uncle Joe bought Black Twist tobacco. It smelt horrible when they smoked it, and they would chew it as well.

On the way back I would pass Wrightson's on one side of Pump Hill and on the other side was Ellerkers. They sold sweets on one side of the shop and veg on the other. Mrs Ellerker made toffee and it was the best toffee ever. She would bring out these wonderful trays filled with nut, treacle and plain toffees. She would have put Thornton's to shame.

She broke it up with a little hammer and it cost 2d a quarter; you got ever such a lot for 1d. They had a son called John, who was the same age as my brother Derek and there was a girl too. Next door to the Ellerkers, my cousin, Nancy Dowson, lived in the house where the Duke of Buckingham died.

The Calams had the King's Head. He was a pigeon-man. When we played with the ball in Nancy's garden it often went over into a paddock at the back of the pub. I never liked going over the wall to get it. Mr Calam wasn't very nice. It was better if we lost the football when playing at the Junior School, cos then we had to get the ball out of the orchard and could pinch some apples at the same time.

Taylor's had a butcher's shop nearly opposite us down an alley between the two little cottages. And I can remember Featherstone's had a big house which backed onto Dale End. There were two large doors which opened onto what had been their dairy and they used to keep butter on the stone shelves cos it was so cold in there.

At the top of the Market Place there was Harry Pierson's farmyard, then a shop. There was a big door which led to the yard. Derek and I would go there, through the double doors, into the yard and up the steps into the granary to get flour. We would bring home a 1-stone bag of white and a ½-stone of wholemeal flour in paper bags. Mum was a good cook and would make dumplings in the oven and finish them off in the pan so they had a crispy top.

I used to hate going past Warren's Farm – Cow Clap Farm I called it. The cows would be brought up the main street from the fields away somewhere and of course when they came to the narrow gate into the farm, they let rip. It stank and I had to dodge past it all to get back home. I never understood all

the names of those who lived there. Warrens owned it, but there were people called Bielby involved somehow. A Mr Bower who also lived there. He used to train horses and kept them in the fields up where Ryedale View is today. That was all orchards and fields in my day.

On the other side was Potter's Farm. They had Italian Prisoners of War working in their fields. We knew which they were, because they had to wear patches on their backs. One man, who everyone called Toni, decided to stay in Kirby after the war finished. He always brought the cows in for Mr Potter and was a little man.

Going up to Potter's farm, on the corner, lived Mr Dale. He would buy rabbit skins from you for 6d. Dad always got given rabbits by the farmers in Gillamoor so we often had skins to sell as well as having roast rabbit with Yorkshire puddings on a Wednesday - "I'm foggy for the skin" was often heard round the house, as we all wanted the 6d!

Mum never had time to go shopping so Derek and I would run all the errands. Suet came from Samuel Waind's butcher's shop opposite Howe End and we always had to have a joint for Sundays. Mum would say to us "Tell Sam I don't want any fix-fax." I can only describe it as solid fat that you couldn't cut or do anything with. So it made the joint weigh more.

Saturday was sheep's head day, which also came from Wainds. Thinking about it now it seems unbelievable, but back then it was wonderful. The large pan would hang on the reckon over the fire and Mum would put in pearl barley

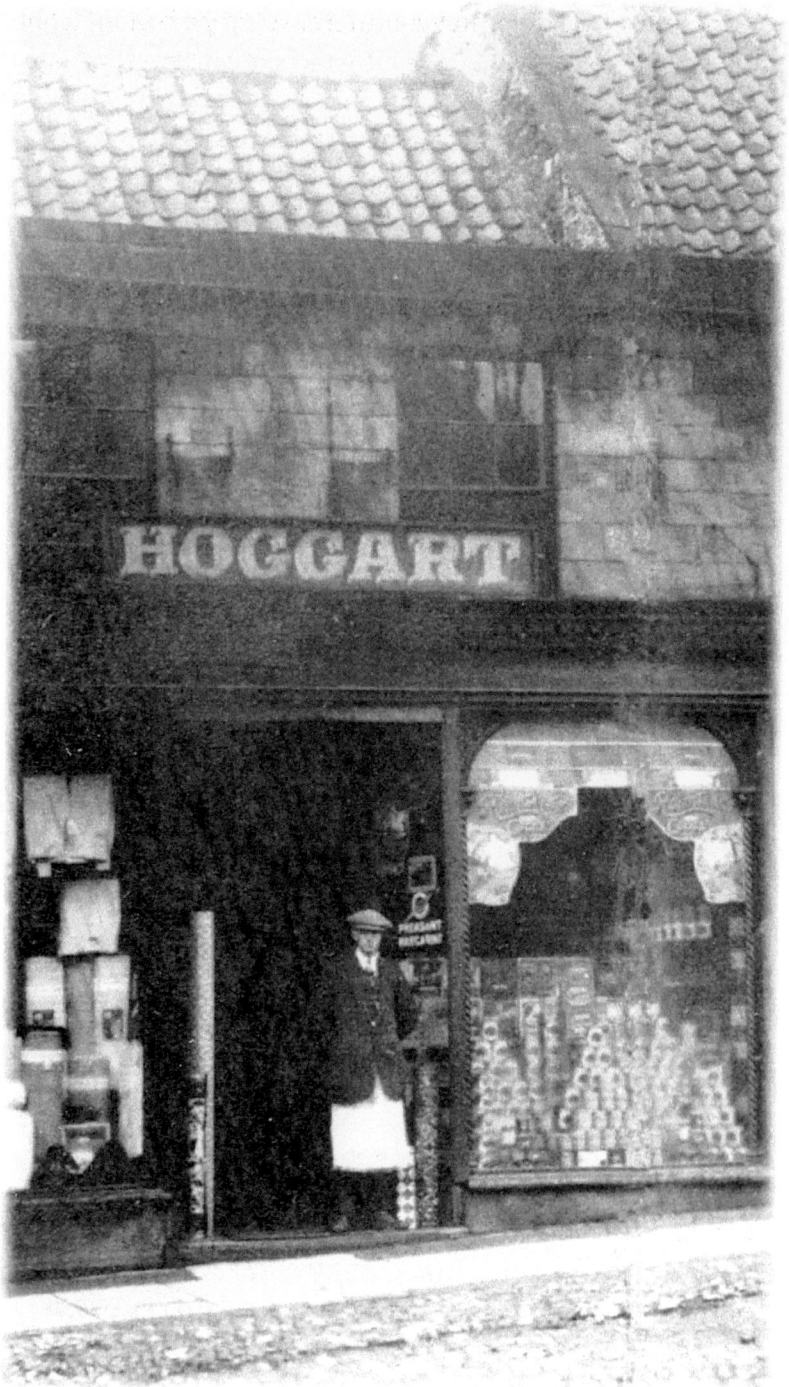

or rice and vegetables and it would cook all day. Mum would add in dumplings as well and it tasted smashing!

We would often be sent to Hoggart's shop. They sold bread and cakes and it was really a family-run business. Isaac and Lilly worked there and we would go and peep in at the window to see who was serving behind the counter before going inside. You see Isaac would give us a little bag of biscuits, iced gems – but Lilly never did.

In Dale End, Hill's had a shop just before Harry Pierson's farm. One side of it was a gentleman's outfitters and the other side sold groceries. I can still see all those cased display boxes, filled with exotic biscuits and glass-topped tins and the treacle, which was dispensed from a tap. It was a wonderful place.

Also in Dale End there was a man named Mr Bowes, who repaired shoes from his house. He married Nellie Cooper – as children we thought them very old to be getting married – although they must only have been in their 20s. He came from Leeds and was lame, so walked with a limp.

In Crown Square there were the hawkers, who sold pots and we went there to buy pot mould. This was the white chalky remains left after the pots had been fired. Mum used to buy it to whiten the stone down the sides of the fire grate and I used to clean the edges of the doorstep with a rub-stone made of it. I would draw patterns on it and Mum would tell me off for making too many shapes. Of course being chalk, it would wash off with the rain.

I can remember Tommy Baker. He had a lorry and would go round selling vases, artificial flowers and such like round the area. He wasn't very clever but was well known. Once when he was asked where he'd been, Tommy replied 'Clear out o't' country' when he'd actually been out to Malton. Another time he was checking his petrol tank to see how much was left in it. In those days, the wagon had a screw top tank at the front which had to be filled up with a funnel. It was only narrow and Tommy couldn't see inside very well. So he lit a match to see and blew his eyebrows off!

Market day in Kirby was always busy. Dad used to come down to meet his travellers from York; one was called Mr Stubbs and Dad bought iron and nails from him. Mr Caldwell travelled over from Scarborough and had a huge fruit and veg stall in the market for years. He used to fill a ½ stone flour bag with a variety of things and sell it for 1/- . If there were no takers, he would add a bag of boiled sweets or a couple of bananas. He was a real salesman and I always had toothache on a Wednesday! Another Scarborough regular was Mr Plewes, who sold fish.

Of course, I can remember when Kirby held the hirings. I loved it, it was so exciting. Corrigan's would come with the penny slot machines and sometimes they brought wild animals in a cage, like a lion, or even an elephant for the fair which set up in the Market Place. The music was fantastic. They had a roundabout, complete with the organ in the centre and animated figures which moved in time to the music. You could hear the music all the way up to Dale End; it was so nice! All the people would come into town from the dales – the lads who came for the hirings would want to take the girls on the roundabout and rides.

My brother Albert, who was 15 years old, would be hired again here. He earned about £5 a year as a farm hand with Mr Cussons down at Ings dairy farm, but his money only came to him at the end of the year. In the meantime Mum would get me to go and ask to borrow money from my sister Hilda. She worked for the doctor so her money was her own. I would have to beg for sixpence for Albert and she would always complain "What again, Albert wants another sixpence?!" For sixpence you could go to the cinema for 4d and then have 2d left for a packet of woodbines.

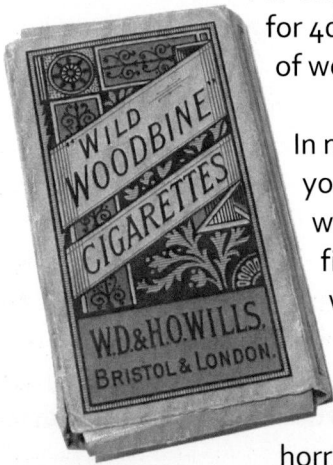

In my day the first thing you did when you left school was start smoking. It was the first thing bought out of your first pay packet – a packet of woodbines. I remember my friend Nora; she was a year older than me and so when she bought a packet, she gave me one to try. It was horrible and I didn't even know whether to suck or blow! What's more, I was terrified my mum would smell the smoke on me, so I chewed a piece of orange peel all the way home.

Mr King used to go to the station every day for the papers and Billy Kips – Mr Hutchinson - went twice a week to collect kippers which he sold to regular customers.

There was Rutter's - the grocery shop in the Church Street. They were real gentry and the shop had a large bay window. Mary, their daughter, was my friend and she used to sit in the window and catch me as I went past. We often used to go down to the tennis courts to watch them play; about where the cricket field is now. I remember she had beautiful hair and I was always jealous of it. I had Dowson hair – wispy. Her parents were always well spoken but rather protective of her.

Mr Hill the watch maker was Mary's uncle so he must have been brother to Mrs Rutter.

I can remember the Bellman of Kirby. We used to follow him as he went round town and listen to his cries. He was really tall, about 6ft, but had two left feet. He wore two left shoes anyway, and always had cut the ends out so his toes poked out. He would turn around and make squeaky voices at us.

Kirby used to have horse fairs, but I can't remember much other than the gypsies bringing the horses to town to trade.

Friends and Neighbours

I can remember almost everyone who lived in Dale End. From the top of Gillamoor Road towards the Market Place there was:

- Mrs Booth or Grannie Booth as we called her, no idea why. She had a daughter - Violet or Ivy - some plant name...
- The Hewitts - Dorothy was one of them, I can't remember who else
- Fannie and Hoppie Sleightholme - they were brother and sister
- The Harrisons - Mrs Harrison did Mum's washing for her when she had another baby. Mum had a baby every two years.

In the straight row, down from Gillamoor Road, there was :
- Mrs Duck
- Then there was a strange three-cornered building where the two Miss Hutchinsons lived
- The Bumby's - there was Mary, Walter and Eva.
- Down Bumby's Hill (down in Manor Vale Lane) there were the Taylors; they had a nice house and it had the gate into the Manor Vale. Mr Taylor was the butcher and they kept pigs down there.
- Lealmans; they had the rope walk in the Vale.

From our corner of Dale End:
- Mr & Mrs Russell - they always had a minister lodging with them as they were Wesleyans. That house was built of brick; not stone.
- Us - the Dowson family
- The Winspears - they were nice, sedate people. Miss Winspear lived with her mother. We always thought she was a spinster but her fellow had gone abroad, India I

think, to make his fortune. Mr Armitage they called him and he did come back for her. He built the house on West Fields - it stood back from the main road, on its own, near to where the school is today. [Broadacres Farm]

- Betsie Bowes - she was a fantastic dressmaker.
- Granny Ward - she brought up her grand-daughter, Lily, after her mum, Granny Ward's daughter, died in childbirth. I think Lily went to live in Scotland last I heard.
- The Wares - Gwennie was my best friend and her dad Mr Ware, worked for Leadley's as a tailor. I remember their house was always tidy, not like ours with washing and ironing always about and a pan on the fire. I would go round to play with her on a night cos she was lonely being an only child. There were plenty of us to go round!

- Mrs & Miss Reveley and Captain Scott Hopkins - they all lived at Low Hall

Captain Scott-Hopkins was their lodger, but as a child I always thought he owned the place; he acted like he did. He had these Jack Russell terriers that ran at you, barking; I was frightened of them. My older sister worked there when she left school and I used to be paid to bring milk from Cussons'

High Market Place, Kirkbymoorside

Town Farm, a jug in each hand, morning and evening. I was eight at the time. Old Mrs Reveley thought I was lovely and she would ask me to go sit on her knee. I remember thinking "I'm too old to be sitting on knees, I'm eight. I put my sisters to bed on a night!" In our house only babies sat on knees. Nevertheless I used to sit there, stiff as a board on the edge of her knees. But she was a nice old lady, real gentry. Later on Miss Reveley moved down into Piercy End and lived in the house opposite Auntie Jinnie's shop.

- Mrs Wrightson - she was on her own when I lived in Dale End. Then the Cook family came to live there, when they left Farndale. Mr Cook started with a horse and cart selling coal and ended up in a business partnership with an oil man from Scarborough.

On the opposite side of Dale End it has all changed; so many of the houses have gone. On the Back Lane there was a doorway opposite us on the corner, which led up into the fields and on to the Union Workhouse. Urgh! We never went up there. But a little further there was a small bungalow:
- Paul Sonley and his wife and children - Ivy, Maggie and Charlie - they lived there. It was a lovely little house on two levels with a garden that joined onto the others and went through into Back Lane.
- Next was a really large garden which had William pear trees which hung over onto the Gillamoor Road. We would throw stones at the pears to knock them down.

Opposite our house there was the entrance to the New Trod which went down the side of the orchard. It had Victoria plums hanging over which we pinched. The New Trod took you straight into Tinley Garth, round the back of the Congregational Chapel.

- Featherstones had the big house (now gone) and next to it were two small cottages set back, I can't remember who was there. But it was round the back of these you went to Mr Taylor for meat.
- Fuzzy Fletcher and Mary Boysey had the next two tall houses. He was a music teacher and led the church choir.
- Mr & Mrs Wilson - and Joan and Muriel, their daughters. He was the Wesleyan Minister who committed suicide. But in those days everyone knew everything - people talked to one another in the streets and no-one had a telephone so had to go for help themselves. My brain has always seen things literally. So when Mum heard the terrible tragedy of Mr Wilson 'putting his head in the oven' I thought they meant a baking oven. I had never seen a gas oven and didn't know the dangers and how it could kill – and so I always thought he had baked himself somehow. Shame - he was a nice little dapper fellow.

- Next to them was someone who drove a petrol wagon. Harold Cram lived there after him (right). The house had a couple of steps up to it.
- Miss Bowes - we never really saw her. She was very posh and had a boyfriend who had a motorbike. 'Bowman Tassio' was what I heard people call him. I think he might have been a lodger at one point. I know everyone complained about the noise his bike used to make roaring down the street.
- Mr & Mrs Harrison - he was a fireman. I remember whenever there was a fire we would go and rush to watch as they brought the horse and cart with the extinguisher; usually by that time the fire had burnt the house down.

- Granny Atkinson - she was grandmother to the Atkinson children, who lived at the Gatehouse near Kirkdale - there was Walter, Bob and Olive.
- Sugary Anna - that's what we called her. Her real name was Hodgson. She was a little wizened old lady with glasses. The kids were always playing tricks on her - I do feel bad about that - aren't children cruel?
- Mr & Mrs Booth - he was a chimney sweep
- Lishmans
- Hills - they had the shop; some lived there and some lived opposite at the bottom of Castlegate near the blacksmith's shop.

Bill Hodgson next to the forge at the bottom of Castlegate

School Days

I went to Kirby School down in Tinley Garth. There was the Infants School, then the Junior School and Senior School. The Infants was next door to the Congregational Chapel and between the Junior and Senior was the police station.

I remember it was Sergeant Gatenby living there around the time I left school because I was friends with his daughter Vera; they had come from Newton. PC Cowse used to live in the little house in Tinley Garth directly opposite the station; he went onto Helmsley and then to Lastingham. PC Barr also lived in that house as well at some point. Kirby had two policemen in town and the sergeant always lived at the station with the constable in the house opposite.

One time Vera's parents went away and there was a relief policeman covering the town. Vera had started work so had to stay and she asked if I would come over and stay with her cos she didn't want to be home alone. Really I wasn't supposed to be there; she never told her parents about me sleeping over and I had to keep out of sight.

The stairs came down into the hall and the office was at the front with bars over the window. During the evening the phone rang, so Vera and I went in to answer it but she didn't put the lights on. Whilst we were there we heard the door opening and I quickly backed up against the wall and stood still. The relief policeman walked in, picked up some paperwork, turned and left. He never saw me and I was only a foot or so away from him.

So much for being a policeman if he didn't see me! I was shaking like a leaf.

I loved being at school. Mrs Smailes was the head teacher and we had Miss Lewin, she was there for years. Miss Fox was a wonderful lady; she always wore a white blouse with a white bow. She married Tar Hodgson.

There were about 30 of us in the class and I can remember we used to make fun of Miss Cole, who came from Gillamoor. She always wore long knickers with elastic round the bottom of the legs. Whenever she reached up to write on the blackboard, her dress would lift up and everyone could see them. It was hilarious. She went on to teach at Pickering School before she retired and moved to Ings Lane.

I went to school with Rene Cossins; she would be Derek Cossin's auntie. We went through school together and it was either Rene or me who would be top of the form. One year I would beat her, the next she beat me and we were like this from age of 5 to 14 years old. When I came top of the spelling test in Year Seven, our final year at school, Mrs Smailes bought two presents. As the winner I got to choose first. One

Frank Cossins, Rene's father and Derek's
grandfather with Sally the spaniel

present was a brooch, the other a bottle of perfume. As I had never had perfume before I chose that, but thinking back I should have chosen the brooch. I would still have the brooch now and that perfume has long gone. Never mind.

I loved lessons; reading, writing and arithmetic. At the age of seven I entered Ryedale Show and wrote a piece about a horse galloping. It was beautifully written out in ink pen on foolscap paper and I won first prize and got three shillings. I was ever so proud. I remember we went after 4 o'clock, because then entry was free. Mum kept it for years, but it got thrown away eventually. I really should have saved it – looking back, I couldn't believe I had written it as a child.

Kirby School had a good name and everyone got a good education. I won second prize for a piece of sewing the following year; I made an apron for Ruby who was just a toddler then. I knew that if Mum had had enough money to buy me some nice material I would have come first. I only had a piece of seersucker and it didn't show the sewing. Mum just didn't have any spare money for things like that.

In Standard Six we were taught to use the sewing machines, but Mum had already taught us that at home so the teachers would send for me to help. I would show the others how to thread the machines and how to work them.

Rene and I used to do all sorts for the teachers, we would be about 10 years old; I remember embroidering these white runners for dressing tables. I did roses and René did water lilies, which were cut out and edged with blanket stitch. I suppose this was part of our lessons really. Miss Beck asked me to make her a camisole, it had lace butterflies in the middle and blanket stitch round the edges and a v-shaped back. I don't know why I did it, cos I really hated her. She used to dig you in the back with a ruler during lessons.

It was all women in our school apart from the Headmaster Mr Donkin and a pupil teacher, Mr Harry Rickaby. He was lovely. His mother used to have people stay quite often and one time she asked if I would come and help her serve meals and fetch things for them. She already had Annie Denney as her cleaner so I was there as an extra pair of hands. I got paid for doing two weeks work. Harry Rickaby was home on holiday from college and he had a microscope in his room. He would show me what things looked like. I remember looking at some cheese through it – it was fascinating. He gave me a watch as well – it was second-hand to him, but I was so proud of it. We didn't have a lot at home.

Harry Rickaby

The Headmaster Mr Donkin was a horrible man. He could be really nice and then turn and be horrible in a split second. He used to knock the lads about, including my brother Albert, for no reason other than he could. He had two sons, who he bullied, and a daughter, Mary, who had Downs Syndrome. He used to make fun of her in front of everyone. I hated him for that – I never could stand for people being ridiculed.

He also picked on a lad from Great Edstone, who had suffered from rickets as an infant. This boy used to walk in every day and by the time he got to school, he was struggling. Mr Donkin used to make him march round the playground for P.E. even though he was in pain. Fred Scaling and Bertie

School garden, Tinley Garth, Kirkbymoorside

Kirkbymoorside Primary School, around 1920

Richardson also were picked on by Mr Donkin and they came from Great Edstone as well. But I did hear that this lad had done really well for himself in America, which was great.

Mr Donkin's sons got revenge on their father though. He would always go through the trod from Piercy End to get to school and one day they strung a rope across it. He got caught and flung back, breaking his ankle; so the school was free of him for six weeks whilst it healed.

We had music lessons and I had a nice singing voice. We used to sing 'Sweet Lass of Richmond Hill' and another was 'Drink to Me Only With Thine Eyes'. The first song every morning would be 'New Every Morning is the Love' and at the end of the day we sang 'Now the Day is Over'. I always thought that was a waste of time, as we all knew the day was over, without singing about it!

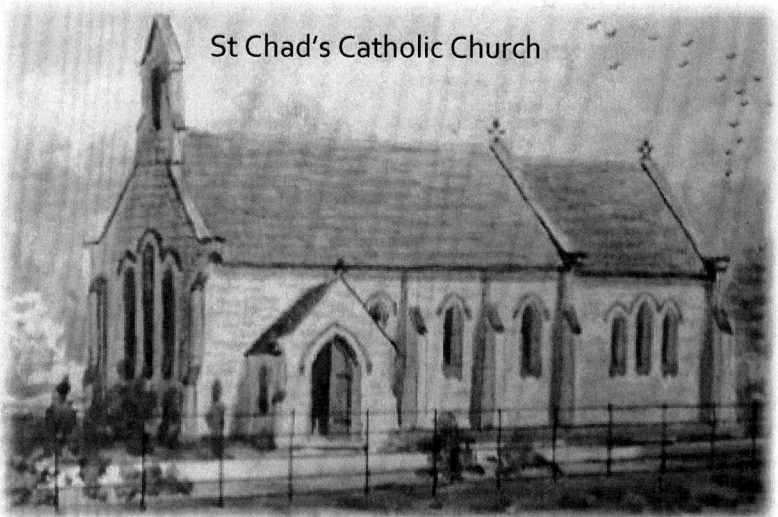
St Chad's Catholic Church

The first lesson of the day after assembly was scripture. So boring. I always wished I was a Catholic then, because they didn't have to do scripture and got to read out the Golden

Treasury storybook instead, which was much more fun. There were only a few Catholics at our school. I remember May Pilmoor and Mary Conning, who were same age as my sister Hilda; there was also Jo and Tom, but maybe they went to the convent school at Pickering instead.

We had a fantastic cookery teacher – Miss MacKenzie, who was Scottish. She used to shout "Keep over Girls" in a broad Scottish accent when she was carrying things out of the oven. We had cookery lessons on a Thursday and we would make dinners in the gas oven in a morning and cakes or bread in the afternoon in the coal oven.

We used Standard Seven's classroom and the shutters were drawn to divide it into two. In the room were two long benches, with vices fitted to them for the boys to do their woodworking lessons. On a Thursday we had to pack all the tools and vices inside the benches, and turn the tops over so the other side could be used for baking.

It was a full day's cooking. In the morning two of us would go to the shops to buy the ingredients for the dinner, such as a meat pie. Once we'd finished, we had to work out the cost of all the ingredients and divide them up and we could buy the food back at cost price. We made some lovely dinners. Once Miss MacKenzie decided to show us how to make custard and she used a glass jug. She put a spoon in and told us this was how to stop the glass cracking when you added the boiling water. But as soon as she poured in the water, it shattered. She screamed and was adamant 'That never happens. It must have been the wrong sort of spoon!'

I remember Miss MacKenzie always wore a white muslin head-dress whilst cooking and she would show us how to wash, iron and starch it. She even brought in a pair of kid gloves and taught us how to handle and clean them. You have to wash them in soap first, then rinse them out and then rub in more soap which you left in to dry. This is how they stayed so soft. She used to go round all the area, giving cookery lessons to Pickering on a Monday and Helmsley School on a Friday. She gave me a good start in life and I still bake coffee cakes for the Scarborough Bowling Club now. Mum never had time to show us how to cook as she was always busy and made everything in such large quantities.

The Tetley residence - Kurnool - now David Begg offices in West End. Mrs Tetley with their driver Mr Underwood

We never had a school nurse come round, because everything had to be paid for in those days. Dr Tetley was our doctor and my sister Hilda worked for him. They had a nanny, parlour maid, housemaid, cook, kitchen maid and chauffeur. They had a special knife sharpener and cleaner. My job was to put the knives into the slots, fill it with Bath Brick and turn the handle. I loved it.

Their two children, Diana and Edward, didn't go to school and so when I went to visit my sister, we would play in the nursery on the rocking horse; of course they had lots of toys. I remember they let me borrow a book – Peter Pan.

Edward and Diana used to ride to the hounds on hunt days. Once Edward came back home, crying his heart out. He had been out all day and his feet were frozen in the boots. He couldn't bear anyone to touch his feet and it took a long while for them to recover.

Derek and I decided one day to follow the hunt on the first day. We walked all the way onto Sinnington where they always had the first meet, chased around over fields all day and then had to walk back at night. It was about 4 o'clock when we got home and we were famished. We'd not taken anything to eat with us! And we never did see a fox.

We did have school concerts, which were held in the Toll Booth. I can't remember many, but one was a Chinese theme and I had to sing and waft a large fan about whilst performing on stage. I must only have been about seven or eight.

We did have the stables in Kirby still, and that was where we held our school sports day on the fields there. The one thing I remember about that is when Billy Boddy had his head split open.

What happened was Jack Kent who lived down West End threw a stone at Billy. He fell to the ground and they had to fetch a nurse with the horse and trap. When I saw him he had his head bound up tight and me being young thought his head had actually split in two and the bandages were holding it together.

I was sorry to leave school and envied those who could go to the Grammar School, but Mum and Dad just couldn't afford to send us.

Chapel Days

I had to go to the Wesleyan Chapel Sunday School twice on a Sunday, in the chapel eyhling. It was down near Leadley's house, just at the side of the chapel. The interior was beautiful, painted in creams and blues, with a pulpit, a balcony and a choir round, which you got to via a set of wooden stairs. Dad always sang in the choir. The moulding was shaped like flowers, picked out in blue and there was a rose in the centre of the ceiling - also blue.

Pencil sketch by Helen Pierson

The organ was huge and Mr Jennings used to play and later on Laura Cole was the organist as well. I remember sitting at the back of the chapel with Uncle Joe holding my hand. We were at my baby brother's funeral - Thomas; I was about seven and can remember Uncle Joe sitting beside me.

Years later I decided to go and sit in the same place and reminisce – I was disgusted when I went in. It is now more like a school room, full of chairs. It seems when the wooden steps became rickety, they decided to strip everything out as well. We used to sit on those steps in the school room listening to bible stories and I even recall joining the Young Leaguers with Gwennie. I think we raised money for the missionaries in Africa and once sent them some beads. I'm sure they didn't need them, but that's what we sent.

The other chapel – the Congregational Chapel in Tinley Garth – was a strange shape to me. It was square and had an altar wall and all the pews were banked up high against the other wall. I went once with Ivy Sonley, to the anniversary. Strange that Kirby had so many churches and chapels. There were the Congregationals (cons as we called them), Wesleyans, Primitives, Catholics, Church and the Quakers.

Kath's grandfather, Joseph Dowson, leading
the Sunday Chapel Outing around 1910

Mum had a relative who was a Quaker; I think she was called Waring. Mum and I went with her just once to the Meeting House, just after my baby brother died. It was a bit boring for me really because everyone just sat there in silence. And it looked just like a house with a back garden.

With Dad working in Gillamoor we got to go on their anniversaries as well. They had a huge wagon with all the little 'uns sitting in the centre hollow and the other older ones sitting on the wide edges. The horses' manes were plaited with blue, red and white ribbons and all the horse brasses shone.

We would go to Beck House at the bottom of Cropton Bank and have milk and sandwiches in the wagon shade, which was an open-sided shed, used simply as a shelter for the wagons. There would be ropes and swings for us to play on.

For the Kirby Wesleyan Chapel outing we all went to Scarborough on the train; Mum and Dad would go with us. We had tea in the chapel opposite Scarborough train station where Mr Dowson, my uncle, was station master. In Kirby it was Mr Hill – he was a little man. After tea we would take the tram right down to the seafront for 2d. I was so excited the night before I would feel sick.

When I think about Kirby, it was all fields, orchards and farms – haven't times changed!

This is an official press shot of Kathleen on her 80th
birthday, when her family bought her a bicycle.

Kath with Keith and Susan (top)
Bill and Kath (below) together with their children and
grandchildren.

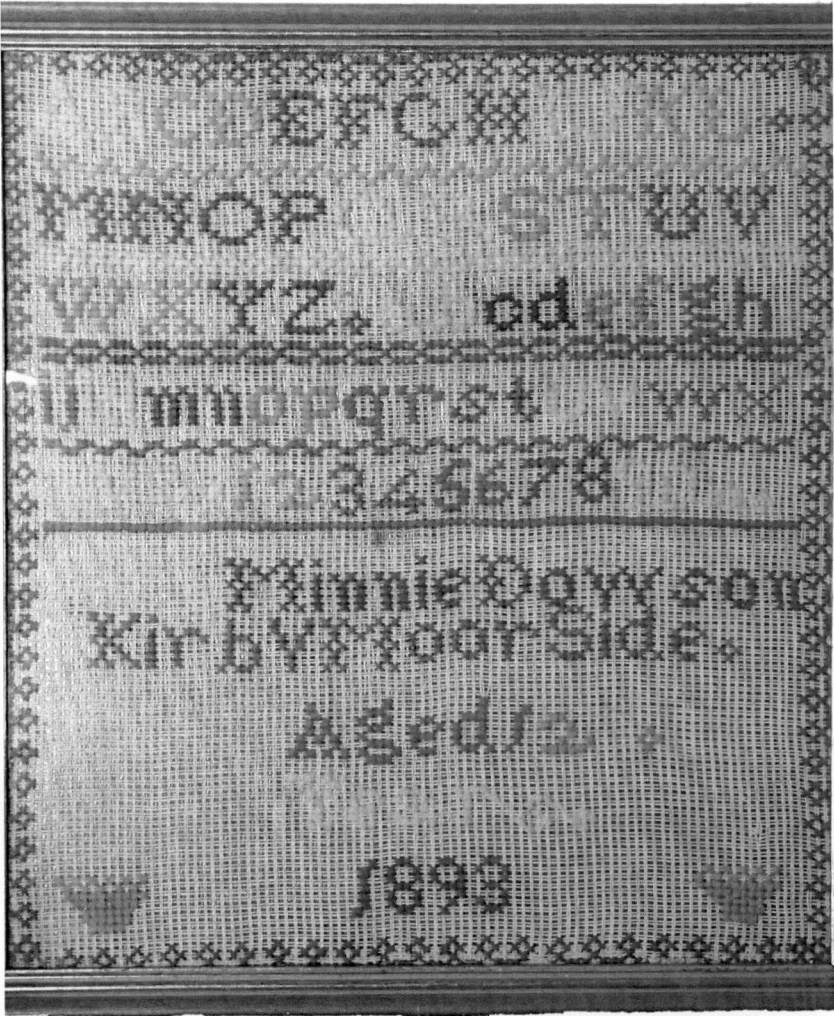

A framed sampler done by Minnie Dowson in 1893 whilst she was suffering from dropsy, a old term used to describe fluid retention, possibly caused by heart problems. Sadly Minnie died a year later, aged just 13.

Dale End: Above in the early 20th century and below in the 21st century.

Joseph Dowson (1850 - 1912)
married
Mary Atkinson (1850 - 1936)

Joseph William (1870 - 1938)

Harriet Jane aka Jinnie (1872 - 1958)

Mary (1874 - 1960)

George (1875 - 1876)

Frederick (1877 - 1947)

Annie (1879 - 1961)

Minnie (1881 - 1894)

Euphemia aka Phoebe (1883 - 1939)

Alice (1885 - 1956)

Emily (1888 - 1900)

George (1892 - 1918)

Thomas (1895 - 1969)

Dowson Family Tree

Joseph & Mary Dowson with their children. Tom and George are at the front. Emily, Alice and Annie are on the left, Joseph and Jinnie are at the back with Fred (Kath's dad); Polly (Mary) and Phoebe on the right.

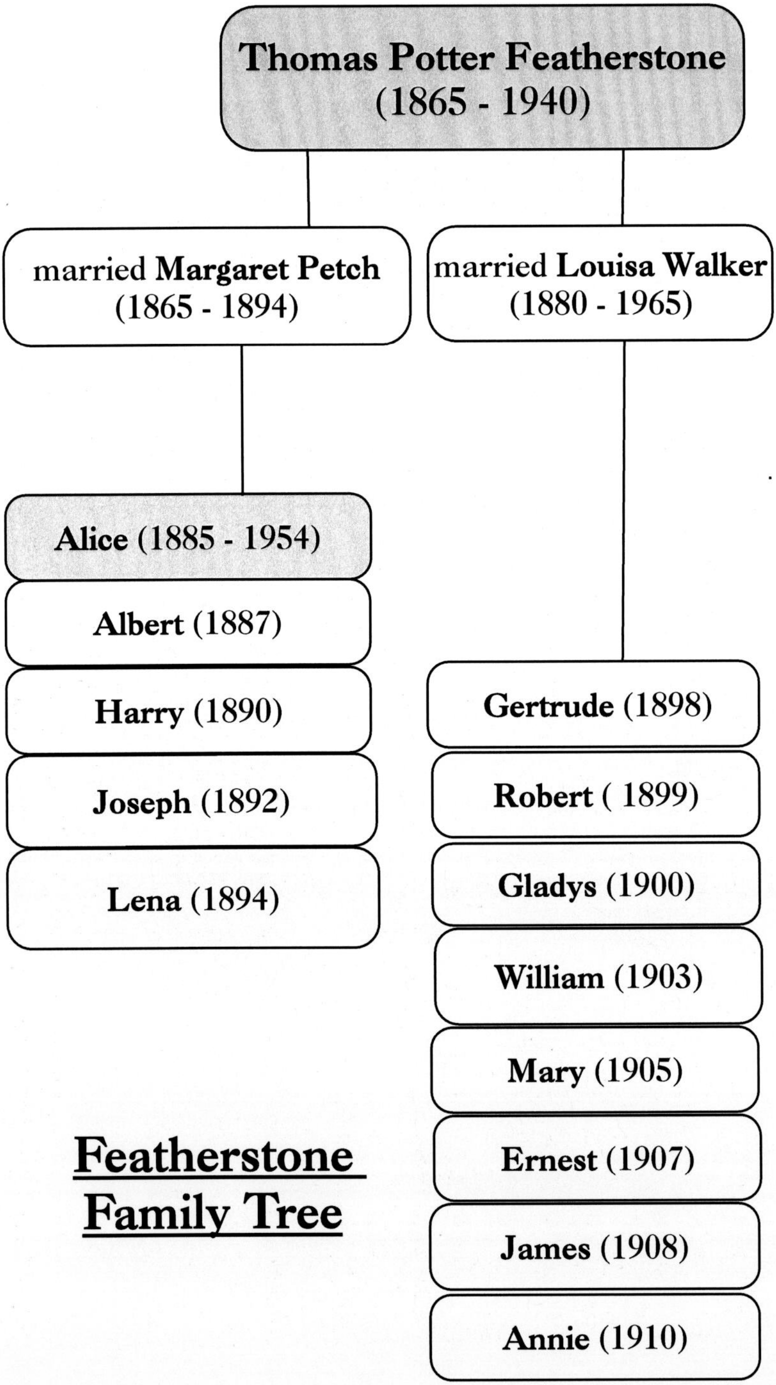

Thomas Potter Featherstone
(1865 - 1940)

married **Margaret Petch**
(1865 - 1894)

married **Louisa Walker**
(1880 - 1965)

Alice (1885 - 1954)

Albert (1887)

Harry (1890)

Joseph (1892)

Lena (1894)

Gertrude (1898)

Robert (1899)

Gladys (1900)

William (1903)

Mary (1905)

Ernest (1907)

James (1908)

Annie (1910)

Featherstone
Family Tree

Thomas Potter Featherstone with his second wife Louisa, holding baby Gladys. Alice is next to her father, with Harry and Gertrude to her right. On the left is Lena, Joseph and brother Albert, who emigrated to Australia. Robert is tucked in front of his father.